Cambridge
Key English Test
2

TEACHER'S BOOK

Examination papers from University of Cambridge ESOL Examinations: English for Speakers of Other Languages

W0230194

CAMBRIDGE
UNIVERSITY PRESS

PUBLISHED BY THE PRESS SYNDICATE OF THE UNIVERSITY OF CAMBRIDGE
The Pitt Building, Trumpington Street, Cambridge, United Kingdom

CAMBRIDGE UNIVERSITY PRESS
The Edinburgh Building, Cambridge CB2 2RU, UK
40 West 20th Street, New York NY 10011–4211, USA
477 Williamstown Road, Port Melbourne, VIC 3207, Australia
Ruiz de Alarcón 13, 28014 Madrid, Spain
Dock House, The Waterfront, Cape Town 8001, South Africa

http://www.cambridge.org

© Cambridge University Press 2003

First published 2001
New edition 2003

Printed in the United Kingdom at the University Press, Cambridge

Typeface: Helvetica 10/13   *System:* QuarkXPress®   [OD&I]

A catalogue record for this book is available from the British Library

ISBN 0 521 52812 7 Student's Book
ISBN 0 521 52813 5 Student's Book with answers
ISBN 0 521 52814 3 Teacher's Book
ISBN 0 521 52815 1 Cassette
ISBN 0 521 52816 X Set of 2 Audio CDs

Contents

Introduction

The background to the update of KET

The Key English Test (KET) was introduced in 1994, following extensive trialling. The examination is now used in over 60 countries. All materials that go into the question papers of KET have been pretested to ensure that they are suitable for the KET candidature and, in terms of difficulty, are at the appropriate level.

As standard practice in Cambridge ESOL, examinations are periodically reviewed as part of the examination production process, to ensure that they remain fair, up-to-date and in line with customer expectations.

As part of the detailed and comprehensive review of the Key English Test which began in 1999, stakeholders were canvassed for opinions on the examination. Teachers, Students, Local Secretaries and Senior Team Leaders provided Cambridge ESOL with valuable feedback about all aspects of KET. We received very encouraging responses from stakeholders around the world, and as a consequence the changes included in the updated tests are minimal. The updated examination in the format in this test book begins in March 2004.

The following summarises the changes to the KET papers.

KET Reading/Writing

- In the old Part 1, questions 1–5 (short signs and notices with three-option multiple-choice format) have been removed
- In the old Part 2, the dictionary definition type matching exercise has been converted into a productive task (Part 6 of the updated test)
- There is a new multiple-choice vocabulary section (Part 2)
- The information transfer exercise (the old Part 7) will sample a wider range of input and output texts in the updated test (Part 8)
- The continuous writing question will become Part 9 in the updated test and candidates will now be required to write 25–35 words (as compared to 20–25 words previously)

KET Listening

No changes

KET Speaking

- The Personal Question Activities will be removed from Part 2 of the test. As a result, all candidates will use the current Non-Personal Question Activity type in Part 2.

The review process leading to the update to KET has been very carefully considered and all new task types have been thoroughly trialled to ensure that the materials are relevant and fair to KET candidates.

The level of KET

Cambridge ESOL has developed a series of examinations which equate to the Council of Europe Common European Framework Language Levels. Within the levels, the Key English Test is at Cambridge Level One and corresponds to the Council of Europe Level A2. This is shown in the chart below.

Cambridge / ALTE Levels   Council of Europe Levels

Cambridge / ALTE Levels		Council of Europe Levels
CPE	Level 5	C2 (Mastery)
CAE	Level 4	C1 (Effective proficiency)
FCE	Level 3	B2 Vantage
PET	Level 2	B1 Threshold
KET & *Flyers*	Level 1	A2 Waystage
Movers Starters		A1 (Break-through)

In the chart, the Main Suite examinations are shown (KET, PET, FCE, CAE and CPE) in capitals and the Young Learner examinations are in italics. KET is approximately the same level as *Flyers*, and both correspond to the Council of Europe Level A2.

Cambridge ESOL is a member of the Association of Language Testers in Europe (ALTE). The members are all providers of examinations in European languages, and one of their principal objectives is to establish a framework of levels of proficiency in order to promote the transnational recognition of certification.

KET offers a basic qualification in English and also represents a first step for those wishing to progress towards Cambridge Level Two, the Preliminary English Test (PET) and other Cambridge ESOL examinations.

Waystage

KET is based on the Council of Europe's *Waystage* document. This represents a level of language ability that should be attainable in 180–200 hours of study. Learners at *Waystage* level possess the basic language skills necessary to cope in predictable situations, with the emphasis on coping with their most urgent communicative needs.

The materials a Waystage user can deal with

A language user at this level needs to be able to read simple texts, many of which are of the kind needed for survival in day-to-day life or while travelling in a foreign country. These include street signs and public notices, product packaging, forms, posters, brochures, city guides and instructions on how to make a phone call. At this level the user can understand the gist of a tourist brochure with the help of a dictionary, to the extent of being able to identify the starting and finishing times of a guided tour and what will be seen on the tour. The user should also be able to deal with personal messages written as letters or postcards, and gain some information from informative texts taken from newspapers and magazines. Where listening skills are concerned, a user needs to understand the basic facts given in announcements such as at railway stations and airports, traffic information given on the radio, public announcements made at sporting events or pop concerts and instructions given by teachers, police, customs officials, etc.

What a Waystage user can do

If studying English in an English-speaking country, a user is able to find out basic information about a language course such as when it starts and how much it costs. If travelling as a tourist, they can understand the outline of the information given on a guided tour, as long as it is in a predictable context, but can ask only very simple questions to get more information. They can express their own likes and dislikes, but only in simple terms.

In the context of work, a language user at this level can handle basic enquiries related to their own familiar job area, dealing, for example, with questions about prices, quantities of goods ordered, or delivery dates. In a meeting, they could provide straightforward facts if asked directly, but cannot follow a discussion. On the telephone, they could take the name of a caller and note down a simple message including a phone number.

They can write very simple personal letters and basic messages, although there may be elementary mistakes.

Preparing for KET

Candidates do not need to follow a specific course before attempting KET. The language skills candidates demonstrate in KET are similar to those they may have to perform in real life situations. Students who have followed any general course for beginners of at least 180–200 learning hours should be able to attempt KET, provided that the course simultaneously develops reading, writing, listening and speaking skills and language resources to the level indicated by *Waystage*, and encourages the use of communication strategies that will enable students to make the most of their limited resources.

Efforts have been made to keep the language of instructions in KET as simple and as clear as possible. However, to ensure that candidates fully understand what they have to do in each part of the test, it is advisable for them to familiarise themselves in advance with the different types of test tasks, as illustrated in the Student's Book. They should also make sure they understand how to record their answers on the answer sheets (see photocopiable samples at the back of the Student's Book).

KET candidates

Information is collected about the KET candidates at each session of the examination, when candidates fill in a Candidate Information Sheet.

In 2001 there were about 40,000 candidates for KET.

The candidate profile for KET in terms of age, educational background and employment/studies varies according to geographical region. The design of questions in KET takes into account the potential diversity of age and linguistic/cultural background of candidates. The majority of KET candidates are in the 11–30 age range.

Nationality

KET is currently available in more than 60 countries around the world. The majority of candidates enter for KET in European and South American countries, and also the Asia-Pacific region. Many candidates also take the exam in the UK and in the Middle East.

Age and gender

In 2001, about 20% of the candidates were 12 and under, about 60% were teenagers, with a further 13% in the 20–29 age range. About 55% of the candidates were female.

Employment

The majority of candidates were full-time students; 18% had a job.

Exam preparation

A large proportion of candidates (about 85%) had attended preparation classes for KET.

Reasons for taking KET

Candidates' reasons for wanting an English language qualification were distributed as follows:

- for personal interest (39%)
- for further study of English (23%)
- for work purposes (28%)
- other reasons (10%)

Language specifications

The language specifications of KET are the same as those set out in *Waystage*. It should be noted that the *Waystage* specification is not a closed syllabus. The following is a summary of the language which is tested in KET. In terms of vocabulary and grammatical structure, KET candidates will have productive control of only the simplest of exponents for each category below; there is a wider, but still limited, range that they will be able to deal with receptively; and they will have strategies for coping with the unfamiliar.

Language purposes

- Carrying out certain transactions:
    Making arrangements
    Making purchases
    Ordering food and drink
- Giving and obtaining factual information:
    Personal
    Non-personal (places, times, etc.)
- Establishing and maintaining social and professional contacts:
    Meeting people
    Extending and receiving invitations
    Proposing/arranging a course of action
    Exchanging information, views, feelings and wishes

Language functions

There are six broad categories of language functions (what people *do* by means of language):

- Imparting and seeking factual information
- Expressing and finding out attitudes
- Getting things done
- Socialising
- Structuring discourse
- Communication repair

Topics

KET candidates will mainly be expected to deal with the personal and the concrete. These include the following topic areas:

- Personal identification
- House, home and environment
- Daily life, work and study
- Free time, sport and entertainment
- Travel and holidays
- Relations with other people
- Health
- Shopping
- Food and drink
- Places
- Language
- Weather

Further information

KET is usually available six times a year on fixed dates in March, May, June (twice), November and December.

Current information on dates and the administrative details of the examination are provided separately to centres. A copy can be obtained from your nearest Cambridge ESOL Examination Centre. A list of Cambridge ESOL Examination Centres is obtainable from Cambridge ESOL (address below) or from the website (address below). All KET entries must be made through an authorised centre.

Further information can be obtained from:

Cambridge ESOL Help Desk
University of Cambridge ESOL Examinations
1 Hills Road
Cambridge, CB1 2EU
UK
Tel: +44 1223 553997
Fax: +44 1223 460278

In some areas this information can be obtained from the British Council.

For up-to-date information on KET and all Cambridge ESOL examinations, visit the website at www.CambridgeESOL.org

KET content and marking

The KET examination consists of Paper 1 (Reading and Writing), Paper 2 (Listening) and Paper 3 (Speaking).

Paper 1	1 hour 10 mins	**Reading and Writing**	9 parts	50% of total
Paper 2	approx 30 mins (including 8 mins transfer time)	**Listening**	5 parts	25% of total
Paper 3	8–10 mins	**Speaking**	2 parts	25% of total

Paper 1   Reading and Writing (1 hour 10 minutes)

In the KET Reading and Writing paper, Parts 1–5 focus on reading and Parts 6–9 focus on writing. There is a total of 56 questions, with an example for each part. The time allowed for this paper is one hour and ten minutes.

Reading texts

Texts vary according to the different test focus of each part. In Parts 1, 4 and 5, texts are authentic but edited to bring vocabulary and structure within the grasp of students at this level. Texts in other parts are specially written but based on authentic types to ensure task authenticity. Texts may contain some vocabulary or structures unknown to candidates, but they will be able to deduce the meaning from the context, and understanding of these words will not be necessary to complete the task. Most texts are short; no text exceeds 230 words.

Part 1   Signs, notices, labels and other very short texts of the type found on roads, in railway stations, airports, shops, restaurants, schools, offices, etc.

Part 2   Simple sentences forming a loose narrative on the same topic, of the type students at this level should be able to read and understand

Part 3   Texts based on the language used in the routine exchanges of daily life

Part 4   Factual text from a newspaper or magazine article, or similar source

Part 5   Factual text from a newspaper or magazine article, junior encyclopaedia or similar source.

Test focus

Part 1   Reading for main message

Part 2   Reading and identifying appropriate vocabulary

Part 3   Reading and identifying appropriate response

Part 4   Reading for main idea(s) and specific detail; making use of interpretation strategies

Part 5   Reading and identifying appropriate structural words

Part 6   Reading and writing down words (focus on vocabulary and spelling)

Part 7   Reading and writing down words (focus on structure and vocabulary)

Part 8   Reading and writing down words (focus on content)

Part 9   Reading and writing a short message (focus on communication of message, appropriacy, accuracy, vocabulary).

Tasks

Part 1   This is a matching task with five questions and eight options to choose between.

Part 2   This is a three-option multiple choice with a lexical focus. There are five questions.

Part 3   There are five multiple-choice questions (each with three options), which require candidates to complete five separate two-line exchanges; these are followed by a matching task with five questions and eight options to choose between, in the context of a short gapped dialogue.

Part 4   The task is either three-option multiple choice, or one involving a choice between Right/Wrong/Doesn't say. There are seven questions.

Part 5   This is a three-option multiple-choice cloze task. There are eight questions.

Part 6   This is a productive task with a lexical testing focus. Five common words are defined and the first letter of the answer is given. Students need to complete the word.

Part 7   This is an open cloze task. Candidates are required to show control of structure and vocabulary in the context of a short letter (or two short notes) of the kind that students at this level might be expected to write. There are ten questions.

Part 8   This is an information transfer task, requiring candidates to extract relevant information from a short input text and use it to complete some kind of form (for example, sports club membership form, etc.). There are five questions.

Part 9 Candidates are required to show that they can communicate a written message (25–35 words) of an authentic type, for example, a note or postcard to a friend. The instructions indicate the type of message required, who it is for and what kind of information should be included. Alternatively, candidates may be asked to read and respond appropriately to a short note from a friend. Candidates are asked to convey three pieces of information.

Marks

Candidates record their answers in pencil on a separate answer sheet within the time allowed. This involves marking the appropriate lozenge for each question in Parts 1–5, writing one word per question for Parts 6 and 7, writing a word, figure or phrase for each question in Part 8 and writing the note or other message asked for in Part 9 (see the photocopiable sample answer sheets at the back of the Student's Book).

One mark is given for each correct answer in Parts 1–8. Correct spelling is required in Parts 6, 7 and 8. There are 5 marks for Part 9 (see below for more details). The total score of a possible 60 marks is then weighted to 50% of the marks available over the whole test.

Assessment of Part 9

An impression mark is awarded to each piece of writing using the criteria shown in the mark scheme on page 10.

Candidates are expected to write a coherent message which clearly conveys all the pieces of information indicated in the instructions. Credit is given for reasonably correct grammar, spelling and punctuation, and appropriate use of vocabulary. However, writing at this level is not expected to be error-free and more weight is given to successful communication of the message than to absolute correctness. Where appropriate, candidates should show awareness of the conventions of note-writing by including a salutation and a signature in their note.

The mark scheme is used in conjunction with notes specific to each test. These task-specific notes indicate which three pieces of information the candidate is expected to include in the piece of writing.

\multicolumn{2}{l}{**Outline mark scheme for Part 9**}	
Mark	Criteria
5	All three parts of message clearly communicated. Only minor spelling errors or occasional grammatical errors.
4	All three parts of message communicated. Some errors in spelling, grammar and/or punctuation.
3	All three parts of message attempted. Expression may require interpretation by the reader. **or** Two parts of message are clearly communicated, but one part is unattempted. Only minor spelling errors or occasional grammatical errors.
2	Only two parts of message communicated. Some errors in spelling and grammar. The errors in expression may require patience and interpretation by the reader.
1	Only one part of message communicated.
0	Question unattempted, or totally incomprehensible response.

Candidates are penalised for writing less than the minimum number of words (i.e. fewer than 25) and for ignoring the conventions of note-writing by not providing a suitable opening and close to their notes. They are not penalised for writing too much, though they are not advised to do so.

See the Key for Part 9 of each paper for some sample scripts with task-specific notes and examiner's comments.

Marking

Answers to Parts 1–5 are scanned by computer. Parts 6–9 are double marked by a team of fully trained markers who are closely supervised at every stage.

The marking of Part 9 requires special treatment. After the examination, a meeting is held with the Chief Examiner in which sample scripts are chosen to demonstrate the range of responses and different levels of competence achieved in the writing task. Task-specific notes to go with the mark scheme are then drawn up. These sample scripts and task-specific notes are used to establish a common standard of assessment for all candidates. Markers refer to the mark scheme and notes throughout the marking process, discussing any problems with the Chief Examiner.

Paper 2 Listening (approx 30 minutes including eight minutes transfer time)

The KET Listening paper is divided into five parts with a total of 25 questions.

The listening texts are recorded on cassette and CD and each text is heard twice. The speed of delivery is at the slower end of the normal speaking speed range. There are pauses for candidates to look at the questions and to make their answers. The instructions to the candidates on the cassette/CD mirror the instructions on the question paper, and there is an example for each part. Candidates put their answers on the question paper as they listen, and they are then given eight minutes at the end of the test to transfer these answers to an answer sheet.

The complete listening test, including time for the transfer of answers, takes about 30 minutes.

Texts

The texts are written or adapted specifically for the test and recorded in a studio to simulate real spoken language. No listening text exceeds 180 words in length.

Part 1   Five separate short dialogues, between two speakers, in informal and neutral contexts.

Part 2   A conversational exchange between two speakers, in an informal context.

Part 3   A conversational exchange between two speakers, possibly a phone conversation, in an informal or neutral context.

Part 4   A dialogue between two people, possibly a phone conversation, in a neutral context.

Part 5   A monologue in a neutral context, possibly a recorded message.

Test focus

Parts 1–3 Listening to identify simple, factual information: for example, prices, times, directions.

Parts 4 and 5   Listening and writing down information.

Tasks

Part 1   There are five multiple-choice questions (each with three options) based on pictures or drawings.

Part 2   This is a matching task with five questions and seven options to choose between. Based on what they hear in the text, candidates have to match, for example, presents to people, or activities to days of the week.

Part 3   There are five multiple-choice questions (each with three options).

Parts 4 and 5   There are five questions in both of these parts. Candidates are required to complete some sort of message, memo or form on the question paper by extracting information from the listening text and writing it down. Information to be written down will consist of numbers, times, dates, prices, words, spellings of names, etc. In each case, candidates will have to write down a figure or one or two words. Recognisable spelling is accepted, except with high frequency words, e.g. *bus*, *red* or if the word has been spelt out.

Marks

One mark is given for each correct answer, making a possible total of 25, or 25% of the whole test.

Marking

Answers to Parts 1–3 are scanned by computer. Parts 4 and 5 are double marked by a team of fully trained markers who are closely supervised at every stage.

Paper 3   Speaking   (8–10 minutes)

The KET Speaking test is conducted by two examiners (an interlocutor and an assessor) with pairs of candidates. The assessor takes no part in the interaction. The Speaking test takes 8–10 minutes for each pair of candidates. Exceptionally, where there is an odd number of candidates at an examining session, the last test of the session will be for a group of three candidates. In this case, the test will last 13–15 minutes.

The Speaking test is divided into two parts. In Part 1, the interaction is between the interlocutor and the candidates, with the interlocutor asking questions from a standardised script. In Part 2, the interaction is between the candidates and is based on scripted instructions and prompt cards. The language of the Speaking test is carefully controlled to be within the grasp of students at this level.

Test focus

- Interacting in conversational English both with an examiner and with a peer (the other candidate)
- Giving and obtaining factual personal information
- Giving and obtaining factual non-personal information
- Giving opinions and feelings on matters relating to personal life, living conditions, occupational activities and leisure activities.

Tasks

Part 1   In this part, each candidate interacts with the interlocutor, using the language normally associated with meeting people for the first time and giving information about things like name, place of origin, occupation and family. This part takes 5–6 minutes.

Part 2   In this part, the two candidates interact with each other. This involves asking and answering questions of a non-personal kind. Prompt cards are used to stimulate questions which will be related to daily life, leisure activities and social life, including references to places, times, facilities, where to go, how to get there, what to eat, etc. Candidates are required to ask and answer about five questions each. This part takes 3–4 minutes.

Assessment and marking

Throughout the Speaking test, candidates are assessed on their language skills, not their personality, intelligence or knowledge of the world. Candidates at this level are not expected to be fluent or accurate speakers, but they are expected to be able to interact and communicate appropriately according to the demands of the test. The language of the Speaking test is carefully controlled to be accessible to candidates at this level. If candidates do not understand a question or an instruction, they should ask for repetition or clarification and they will get credit for using this strategy. Similarly, they will get credit for the use of paraphrase to supplement inadequate linguistic resources. In some cases, a one or two word response is all that is required to a question, but candidates will be given credit for extending their utterances to the phrase or sentence level, where this is appropriate.

The assessor awards a mark for each of the three criteria, while the interlocutor gives a global mark. The Speaking test accounts for 25% of the total marks for the test.

Candidates are assessed on their own individual performance according to the established criteria and are not assessed in relation to each other. In Part 2, where candidates are required to interact with each other, they will get credit for co-operating to negotiate meaning, but one candidate will not be penalised for another's shortcomings.

The marks given for the whole test are awarded on the basis of the following criteria.

Grammar and vocabulary

This refers to the ability to use vocabulary, structure and paraphrase strategies to convey meaning. Candidates at this level are only expected to have limited linguistic resources, and it is success in using these limited resources to communicate a message which is being assessed rather than range and accuracy.

Pronunciation

This refers to the intelligibility of the candidate's speech. First language interference is expected and not penalised if it does not affect communication.

Interactive communication

This refers to the ability to take part in the interaction, with the examiner and the other candidate, appropriately and with a reasonable degree of fluency. Hesitations while the candidate searches for language are expected and not penalised so long as they do not strain the patience of the listener. Candidates should also display the ability to ask for repetition or clarification, if necessary.

Standardisation

All oral examiners are fully trained so that they conduct the Speaking test and award marks in a standardised way. After initial recruitment, induction and training, standardisation of procedure and assessment is maintained both by attendance at regular co-ordination sessions and by monitoring visits to centres by Team Leaders.

In most countries, oral examiners are assigned to teams, each of which is led by a Team Leader, who gives advice and support to examiners as required. The Team Leaders are responsible to a Senior Team Leader who is the professional representative of Cambridge ESOL for the oral examinations. Senior Team Leaders are appointed by Cambridge ESOL and attend co-ordination and development sessions in the UK. Team Leaders are appointed by the Senior Team Leader in consultation with the local administration.

Grading, awards and results

Grading

Grading takes place once all answer sheets and mark sheets have been returned to Cambridge ESOL and marking is complete. This is approximately four weeks after the examination.

The final grade boundaries are set using the following information:
- information on the difficulty level of individual items and the components as a whole (from pretesting information and the use of anchor tests)
- data on the candidates
- data on the overall candidate performance
- statistics on individual items, for those parts of the examination for which this is appropriate (Papers 1 and 2).

A candidate's overall KET grade is based on the aggregate score gained by the candidate across all three papers.

Grade Review takes place immediately after Grading. All candidates who have failed the examination by a very small margin have their Writing Component mark checked.

Special Circumstances

Special Circumstances covers three main areas: Special Arrangements, Special Consideration and Malpractice.

Special Arrangements: These are available for candidates with a long term disability such as hearing/sight impairment, dyslexia or a speech impediment, or short term difficulties such as a broken arm. They may include extra time, separate accommodation or equipment, Braille transcription, etc. Consult the Cambridge ESOL Local Secretary in your area for more details.

Special Consideration: Cambridge ESOL may give Special Consideration to candidates affected by adverse circumstances immediately before or during an examination. Applications for Special Consideration are submitted by centres and must be made within two weeks of the examination date.

Malpractice: The Malpractice Committee will consider cases where candidates are suspected of copying or collusion, or where other breaches of exam regulations are reported. Results may be withheld pending further investigation. Centres are notified if a candidate is suspected of malpractice.

Results

Statements of Results are usually sent out about five or six weeks after the date of the examination. Results are reported in the following way: there are two pass grades ('Pass with Merit' and 'Pass'), and two fail grades ('Narrow Fail' and 'Fail').

Pass with Merit ordinarily corresponds to a mark of 85% and above in the examination. Pass usually represents a mark of between 70–85%. A Narrow Fail result indicates that the candidate was within 5% of the Pass boundary.

Each candidate is provided with a Statement of Results which includes a graphical display of the candidate's performance in each paper. These are shown against the scale Exceptional–Good–Borderline–Weak and indicate the candidate's relative performance in each paper.

Certificates are sent to candidates achieving one of the pass grades within six weeks of the despatch of Statements of Results.

Paper 3 frames

Test 1

Note: The visual material for Paper 3 appears on pages 74–81 of the Student's Book.

Part 1 (5–6 minutes)

Greetings and introductions

At the beginning of Part 1, the interlocutor greets the candidates, asks for their names and asks them to spell something.

Giving information about place of origin, occupation, studies

The interlocutor asks the candidates about where they come from/live, and for information about their school/studies/work.

Giving general information about self

The interlocutor asks candidates questions about their daily life, past experiences or future plans. They may be asked, for example, about their likes and dislikes or about recent past experiences, or to describe and compare places.

Extended response

In the final section of Part 1, candidates are expected to give an extended response to a 'Tell me something about …' prompt. The topics are still of a personal and concrete nature. Candidates should produce at least three utterances in their extended response.

Part 2 (3–4 minutes)

The interlocutor introduces the activity as follows:

Interlocutor: *(Pablo)* here is some information about a dentist.

(Interlocutor shows answer card 1A on page 74 of the Student's Book to Pablo.)

(Laura) you don't know anything about the dentist, so ask *(Pablo)* some questions about it.

(Interlocutor shows question card 1B on page 75 of the Student's Book to Laura.)

Use these words to help you. *(Interlocutor indicates prompt words.)*

Do you understand?

Now *(Laura)* ask *(Pablo)* your questions about the dentist and *(Pablo)* you answer them.

1A

Mary Brown

DENTIST

17, Mount Street

For appointments Tel: 980 4723

Opening times: Monday–Thursday 12.30–8 p.m.

Car parking in Water Lane

1B

DENTIST

◆ **name?**

◆ **telephone number?**

◆ **appointment / evening?**

◆ **address?**

◆ **car park?**

When the candidates have asked and answered their questions about the dentist, they then exchange roles and talk about a different topic.

The interlocutor introduces the activity as follows:

Interlocutor: *(Laura)* here is some information about a new shopping centre.

(Interlocutor shows answer card 1C on page 75 of the Student's Book to Laura.)

(Pablo) you don't know anything about the shopping centre, so ask *(Laura)* some questions about it.

(Interlocutor shows question card 1D on page 74 of the Student's Book to Pablo.)

Use these words to help you. *(Interlocutor indicates prompt words.)*

Do you understand?

Now *(Pablo)* ask *(Laura)* your questions about the shopping centre and *(Laura)* you answer them.

1C

WESTWOOD SHOPPING CENTRE
opens next month!

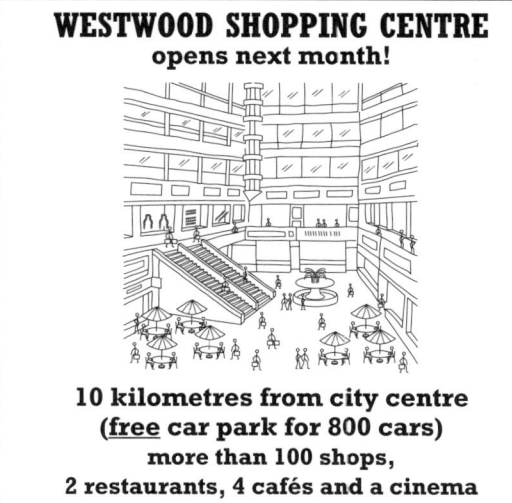

**10 kilometres from city centre
(<u>free</u> car park for 800 cars)
more than 100 shops,
2 restaurants, 4 cafés and a cinema**

1D

NEW SHOPPING CENTRE

◆ name?

◆ where?

◆ many shops?

◆ car park?

◆ open today?

Note: Candidates are assessed on both their questions and answers in Part 2 of the test.

Test 2

Note: The visual material for Paper 3 appears on pages 74–81 of the Student's Book.

Part 1 (5–6 minutes)

Greetings and introductions

At the beginning of Part 1, the interlocutor greets the candidates, asks for their names and asks them to spell something.

Giving information about place of origin, occupation, studies

The interlocutor asks the candidates about where they come from/live, and for information about their school/studies/work.

Giving general information about self

The interlocutor asks candidates questions about their daily life, past experiences or future plans. They may be asked, for example, about their likes and dislikes or about recent past experiences, or to describe and compare places.

Extended response

In the final section of Part 1, candidates are expected to give an extended response to a 'Tell me something about …' prompt. The topics are still of a personal and concrete nature. Candidates should produce at least three utterances in their extended response.

Part 2 (3–4 minutes)

The interlocutor introduces the activity as follows:

Interlocutor: *(Pablo)* here is some information about an international library.

(Interlocutor shows answer card 2A on page 76 of the Student's Book to Pablo.)

(Laura) you don't know anything about the library, so ask *(Pablo)* some questions about it.

(Interlocutor shows question card 2B on page 77 of the Student's Book to Laura.)

Use these words to help you. *(Interlocutor indicates prompt words.)*

Do you understand?

Now *(Laura)* ask *(Pablo)* your questions about the library and *(Pablo)* you answer them.

2A

INTERNATIONAL LIBRARY

BOOKS, CDs
AND VIDEOS

*OVER 100 FOREIGN
NEWSPAPERS AND
MAGAZINES*

ENTRANCE FREE
Monday – Saturday 9.30 a.m. – 6 p.m.
New England House, Museum Street

2B

LIBRARY

◆ **where?**

◆ **close?**

◆ **open / Sunday?**

◆ **cost? £**

◆ **foreign magazines?**

When the candidates have asked and answered their questions about the library, they
then exchange roles and talk about a different topic.

The interlocutor introduces the activity as follows:

Interlocutor: *(Laura)* here is some information about a holiday sports club.

*(Interlocutor shows answer card 2C on page 77 of the Student's Book to
Laura.)*

(Pablo) you don't know anything about the sports club, so ask *(Laura)*
some questions about it.

*(Interlocutor shows question card 2D on page 76 of the Student's Book
to Pablo.)*

Use these words to help you. *(Interlocutor indicates prompt words.)*

Do you understand?

Now *(Pablo)* ask *(Laura)* your questions about the sports club and
(Laura) you answer them.

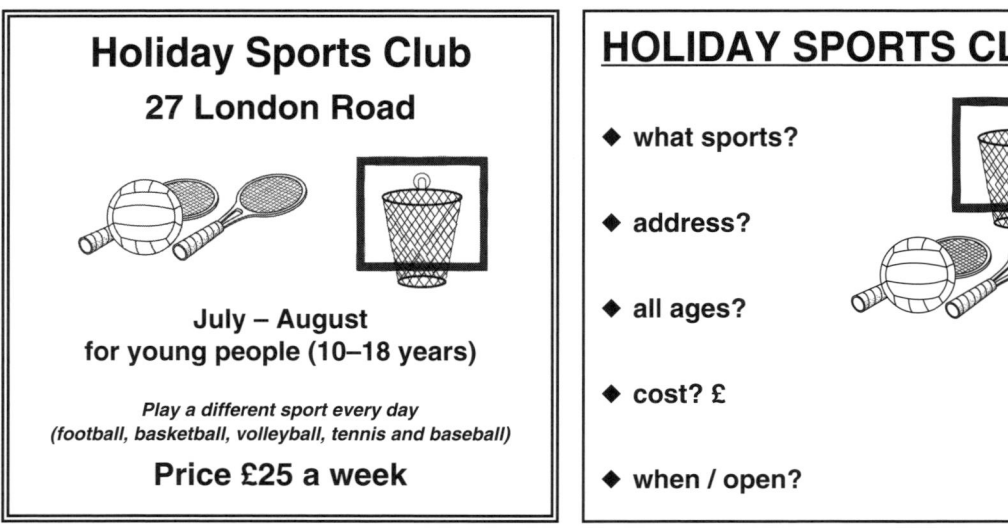

2C

Holiday Sports Club
27 London Road

July – August
for young people (10–18 years)

*Play a different sport every day
(football, basketball, volleyball, tennis and baseball)*

Price £25 a week

2D

HOLIDAY SPORTS CLUB

◆ **what sports?**

◆ **address?**

◆ **all ages?**

◆ **cost? £**

◆ **when / open?**

Note: Candidates are assessed on both their questions and answers in Part 2 of the test.

Test 3

Note: The visual material for Paper 3 appears on pages 74–81 of the Student's Book.

Part 1 (5–6 minutes)

Greetings and introductions

At the beginning of Part 1, the interlocutor greets the candidates, asks for their names and asks them to spell something.

Giving information about place of origin, occupation, studies

The interlocutor asks the candidates about where they come from/live, and for information about their school/studies/work.

Giving general information about self

The interlocutor asks candidates questions about their daily life, past experiences or future plans. They may be asked, for example, about their likes and dislikes or about recent past experiences, or to describe and compare places.

Extended response

In the final section of Part 1, candidates are expected to give an extended response to a 'Tell me something about …' prompt. The topics are still of a personal and concrete nature. Candidates should produce at least three utterances in their extended response.

Part 2 (3–4 minutes)

The interlocutor introduces the activity as follows:

Interlocutor: *(Pablo)* here is some information about a lake.

(Interlocutor shows answer card 3A on page 78 of the Student's Book to Pablo.)

(Laura) you don't know anything about the lake, so ask *(Pablo)* some questions about it.

Interlocutor shows question card 3B on page 79 of the Student's Book to Laura.)

Use these words to help you. *(Interlocutor indicates prompt words.)*

Do you understand?

Now *(Laura)* ask *(Pablo)* your questions about the lake and *(Pablo)* you answer them.

3A

SILVER LAKE

A great place for a holiday

20 kilometres from the city airport
5 large, new hotels
Walking, swimming and boat trips
Dry and sunny 300 days a year

3B

LAKE

◆ **name / lake?**

◆ **where?**

◆ **rain / often?**

◆ **what / do?**

◆ **modern hotels?**

When the candidates have asked and answered their questions about the lake they then exchange roles and talk about a different topic.

The interlocutor introduces the activity as follows:

Interlocutor: *(Laura)* here is some information about an island.

(Interlocutor shows answer card 3C on page 79 of the Student's Book to Laura.)

(Pablo) you don't know anything about the island, so ask *(Laura)* some questions about it.

(Interlocutor shows question card 3D on page 78 of the Student's Book to Pablo.)

Use these words to help you. *(Interlocutor indicates prompt words.)*

Do you understand?

Now *(Pablo)* ask *(Laura)* your questions about the island and *(Laura)* you answer them.

3C

RED SANDS ISLAND

A beautiful island for a special holiday

Sun and blue sky

Hundreds of different birds
Campsite for 50 tents

Boats daily from Port Martin

3D

ISLAND

◆ **name / island?**

◆ **what / see?**

◆ **where / stay?**

◆ **weather?**

◆ **how / get there?**

Note: Candidates are assessed on both their questions and answers in Part 2 of the test.

Test 4

Note: The visual material for Paper 3 appears on pages 74–81 of the Student's Book.

Part 1 (5–6 minutes)

Greetings and introductions

At the beginning of Part 1, the interlocutor greets the candidates, asks for their names and asks them to spell something.

Giving information about place of origin, occupation, studies

The interlocutor asks the candidates about where they come from/live, and for information about their school/studies/work.

Giving general information about self

The interlocutor asks candidates questions about their daily life, past experiences or future plans. They may be asked, for example, about their likes and dislikes or about recent past experiences, or to describe and compare places.

Extended response

In the final section of Part 1, candidates are expected to give an extended response to a 'Tell me something about …' prompt. The topics are still of a personal and concrete nature. Candidates should produce at least three utterances in their extended response.

Part 2 (3–4 minutes)

The interlocutor introduces the activity as follows:

Interlocutor: *(Pablo)* here is some information about a museum.

(Interlocutor shows answer card 4A on page 80 of the Student's Book to Pablo.)

(Laura) you don't know anything about the museum, so ask *(Pablo)* some questions about it.

(Interlocutor shows question card 4B on page 81 of the Student's Book to Laura.)

Use these words to help you. *(Interlocutor indicates prompt words.)*

Do you understand?

Now *(Laura)* ask *(Pablo)* your questions about the museum and *(Pablo)* you answer them.

4A

SANDON AIR MUSEUM

More than 70 aeroplanes to look at
OPEN DAILY 10 a.m.–6 p.m.
Shop with books and postcards
Large free car park

Tickets: Adults £8.00   Students £5.00

4B

MUSEUM

◆ **what / see?**

◆ **open / weekends?**

◆ **student ticket? £**

◆ **car park?**

◆ **buy / postcard?**

When the candidates have asked and answered their questions about the museum they then exchange roles and talk about a different topic.

The interlocutor introduces the activity as follows:

Interlocutor: *(Laura)* here is some information about a bookshop.

(Interlocutor shows answer card 4C on page 81 of the Student's Book to Laura.)

(Pablo) you don't know anything about the bookshop, so ask *(Laura)* some questions about it.

(Interlocutor shows question card 4D on page 80 of the Student's Book to Pablo.)

Use these words to help you. *(Interlocutor indicates prompt words.)*

Do you understand?

Now *(Pablo)* ask *(Laura)* your questions about the bookshop and *(Laura)* you answer them.

4C

WORLD BOOKS

212 Main Street

Largest bookshop in the country

Get your travel books here

Monday–Saturday	10.00 a.m. – 8.00 p.m.
Sunday	12.30 p.m. – 8.00 p.m.

Tel: 724 399

4D

BOOKSHOP

♦ **address?**

♦ **big / small?**

♦ **closed / Sundays?**

♦ **sell / travel books?**

♦ **telephone number?**

Note: Candidates are assessed on both their questions and answers in Part 2 of the test.

Test 1 Key

Paper 1   Reading and Writing

Part 1
1 H   **2** F   **3** E   **4** A   **5** G

Part 2
6 B   **7** C   **8** C   **9** A   **10** B

Part 3
11 C   **12** B   **13** A   **14** B   **15** C
16 B   **17** A   **18** F   **19** H   **20** C

Part 4
21 A   **22** C   **23** B   **24** C   **25** B   **26** B   **27** A

Part 5
28 A   **29** B   **30** A   **31** C   **32** A   **33** B   **34** B   **35** B

Part 6
For questions 36–40, spelling must be correct.
36 uncle   **37** grandmother   **38** wife   **39** aunt   **40** daughter

Part 7
For questions 41–50, ignore capitals/absence of capitals. Spelling must be correct.
41 in   **42** like   **43** much   **44** how   **45** you   **46** on/from
47 costs/is/'s   **48** to   **49** a/one/our/the/another   **50** this/that/it

Part 8
For questions 51–55, spelling must be correct and capitals must be used where necessary.
51 (Mr etc.) (SJ) Renshaw   **52** (on/from) 10(th) April
53 (for) 7/seven days/a/one week   **54** Mary Jones
55 22 King's Road, Weston

Part 9
Question 56
The task-specific notes given below should be used in conjunction with the mark scheme for Part 9 given on page 10.

Task-specific notes
The note should include the following three pieces of information:

i   reason why can't go
ii mention of meeting on another day
iii where you can meet on another day.

Sample answer A

Mark: 5
The three parts of the message are clearly communicated and there are only occasional grammatical errors (*go to the swimming*).

> Dear Lina,
>   I am sorry I can't because I go to the cinema. Can we go to the swimming on Sunday at 6.30 in the evening. If you want to go. come to the bus station on Sunday at 6.00 o'clock.
>   See you later
>   Yours Shida

Sample answer B

Mark: 4
All three parts of the message are communicated but more frequent errors in the structure prevent it from achieving a 5.

> I am sorry Penny for the swimming tomorrows evening. My grandmother she is in the hospital. It's possible for me at Saturday night. We go at disco.
>   Celia

Sample answer C

Mark: 3
The writer has attempted all three parts of the task but the confusion of tense, *viseted*, and use of *last week* rather than *next week* requires interpretation on the part of the reader.

> I'm Sorry my friend. I cant go with you Because I viseted My grand Mother and grand father. Can you meet Last week.
>   See my soon
>   Ali

Sample answer D

Mark: 1

The writer has only covered one part of the message. There are also many errors in both the spelling and the grammar.

> *Dear, Mohan*
> *I'am sory I can not tomorrow go to the sea For swimming.*
> *I'am ill. Now I'am sleep in Hospital. I'am good helth*

Sample answer E

Mark: 0

This is an example of a candidate either not understanding or not following the task.

> *Dear Andre.*
> *Hi I am sorry I don't understand you why you can't go weth me to*
> *Leeds. Do you know when you can go weth me becaus I whant buy*
> *bots call me please.*
> *see you letter by.*

Paper 2 Listening

Part 1
1 B   **2** C   **3** B   **4** B   **5** C

Part 2
6 E   **7** F   **8** A   **9** C   **10** G

Part 3
11 A   **12** C   **13** A   **14** B   **15** A

Part 4
For questions 16–20, ignore capitals/absence of capitals. In question 16, spelling must be correct. For questions 17–20, accept recognisable spelling.
16 HYDE   **17** factory   **18** 11.30/half past eleven/eleven thirty
19 21/twenty-one   **20** photograph(s)/photo(s)

Part 5
For questions 21, 24 and 25, accept recognisable spelling. Spelling of car park *and* pink *needs to be correct.*
21 7.30/half past seven/seven thirty   **22** (big) car park (behind hotel)
23 pink   **24** (the) office   **25** (a) jacket

Transcript

This is the Key English Test. Paper 2. Listening. Test number one. There are five parts to the test. Parts One, Two, Three, Four and Five.

We will now stop for a moment before we start the test. Please ask any questions now because you mustn't speak during the test.

[pause]

PART 1   *Look at the instructions for Part One.*

[pause]

You will hear five short conversations.
You will hear each conversation twice.
There is one question for each conversation.
For questions 1–5, put a tick under the right answer.

Here is an example:
How many people were at the meeting?

Woman: Were there many people at the meeting?
Man: About thirty.
Woman: That's not many.
Man: No, but more than last time.

[pause]

The answer is 30, so there is a tick in box C.
Now we are ready to start.
Look at question one.

[pause]

Question 1   *One*
What will they eat for dinner this evening?

Mother: What do you want for dinner this evening, Maria? We could have pizza … or chicken.
Maria: Mm, what about fish? I had a pizza last night.
Mother: OK. That's easy to cook.
Maria: Good.

[pause]

Now listen again.

[repeat]

[pause]

Question 2   *Two*
What time is it?

Man: Have you got the right time? I think my watch is wrong.
Woman: Er – it's half past two.
Man: Ah – my watch says twenty past.
Woman   Well, it's ten minutes slow then.

[pause]

Now listen again.

[repeat]

[pause]

Question 3   *Three*

What's Michelle going to read?

Man: Can I read your newspaper, Michelle?
Michelle: Didn't you bring a book with you?
Man: Yes, but it's not very interesting.
Michelle: Oh, here you are. I'll read this letter from John.

[pause]

Now listen again.

[repeat]

[pause]

Question 4   *Four*

How much did the tickets cost?

Woman: Oh hi – did you have a good time at the theatre last night?
Man: Well, the play was excellent but the tickets cost ninety dollars each.
Woman: That's not too bad if the play was good.
Man: No, perhaps you're right.

[pause]

Now listen again.

[repeat]

[pause]

Question 5   *Five*

Where is the chemist's?

Man: Excuse me, can you tell me where the chemist's is, please?
Woman: Mm, just a moment. Oh yes! It's past the post office, next to a big
              supermarket.
Man: Is it far from here?
Woman: No, just two minutes' walk.

[pause]

Now listen again.

[repeat]

[pause]

This is the end of Part One.

Now look at Part Two.

[pause]

PART 2   *Listen to Kate telling Emma about her family.*
Where is each person going today?
For questions 6–10, write a letter, A–H, next to each person.
You will hear the conversation twice.

[pause]

Emma: Hi, Kate. What about a game of tennis some time?

Kate: I'd like to Emma, but not today. I'm really busy.

Emma: What are you doing?

Kate: Sam's got toothache so I'm going to take him to the dentist this morning …

Emma: Oh dear!

Kate: … and then mother's going to the hairdresser this afternoon and I said I would drive her home afterwards. Then after school Tanya wants me to help her buy some new shoes. She doesn't like shopping alone.

Emma: My daughter doesn't either. You're going to the concert this evening, aren't you?

Kate: I'm afraid not. But Len loves classical music, so he'll go.

Emma: Oh good. By the way, has Tom started driving yet?

Kate: He's having his first lesson today. He's going to the driving school at lunchtime. He's really excited about it.

Emma: I'm sure he is. How's your father? Does he still play golf?

Kate: No, not any more, but he's started learning Spanish. Actually, he's got a class this evening!

Emma: Good for him. Well, perhaps we can go to the tennis club tomorrow?

Kate: Yes, OK!

[pause]

Now listen again.

[repeat]

[pause]

This is the end of Part Two.
Now look at Part Three.

[pause]

PART 3   *Listen to a woman talking to a policeman.*
For questions 11–15, tick A, B or C.
You will hear the conversation twice.
Look at questions 11–15 now. You have 20 seconds.

[pause]

Now listen to the conversation.

Man: Good morning, madam. Can I help you?

Woman: Yes. I've lost my bag.

Man: Oh, I am sorry. Now, where did you lose it?

Woman: In the town centre. I had it when I got off the bus.

Man: Was there much money in the bag?

Woman: No, there wasn't. I usually have forty or fifty pounds in it, but today I think there was only about twenty.

Man: What else was in the bag?

Woman: Just my gloves. I left my credit card and driving licence at home.
Man: Was the bag expensive?
Woman: No, it was an old one. It wasn't big enough really.
Man: Now, what time did you lose it?
Woman: Well, I left home about nine thirty and the bus takes half an hour, so I lost it about ten o'clock.
Man: Right. Well, I'll phone you tomorrow to tell you if we find it. Are you at home in the afternoon?
Woman: Sorry, I'm going out until the evening. Could you phone before ten in the morning?
Man: Certainly. I'll call then. Now, what's your number?
Woman: It's oh three six two …

[pause]

Now listen again.

[repeat]

[pause]

This is the end of Part Three.
Now look at Part Four.

[pause]

PART 4   *You will hear a man speaking on the telephone.*
He wants to speak to Miss Dixon, but she's not there.
Listen and complete questions 16–20.
You will hear the conversation twice.

[pause]

Woman: Brown's Builders, good afternoon.
Man: Good afternoon. I'd like to speak to Miss Dixon, please.
Woman: I'm afraid she's not in the office at the moment.
Man: Can you give her a message for me?
Woman: Yes, certainly. Who's calling please?
Man: My name is Hyde.
Woman: How do you spell that, please?
Man: That's H-Y-D-E.
Woman: Right, Mr Hyde.
Man: Could you tell her that the time of the meeting has changed?
Woman: Is that the meeting about the new houses?
Man: No, about the new factory.
Woman: I see. And when is it?
Man: It's on Wednesday at half past eleven.
Woman: Does Miss Dixon know where the meeting is?
Man: I think so. It's in our main office. Ask her to go to Room 21.
Woman: Right, I'll tell her.
Man: And could you ask her to bring the photographs with her?
Woman: Which photos do you mean?
Man: She'll know which ones. They're very important.
Woman: Don't worry, I'll tell her. Thank you very much, Mr Hyde.
Man: Thank you. Goodbye.
Woman: Goodbye.

[pause]

Now listen again.

[repeat]

[pause]

This is the end of Part Four.
Now look at Part Five.

[pause]

PART 5   *You will hear a man talking about a day trip.*
Listen and complete questions 21–25.
You will hear the information twice.

[pause]

Tour guide: Ladies and gentlemen. Here's some information about our trip to Loch Ness tomorrow. It's a long journey, about three hours each way, so we have to start early. That means we'll have breakfast at half past seven. Don't be late, please, as the bus has to leave at half past eight. When you finish breakfast, go to the car park. That's where we'll get on the bus. That's the big car park behind the hotel. Remember to bring your pink tickets for lunch. We'll have lunch at a restaurant near Loch Ness and you must have your pink ticket or you won't get any lunch! If you haven't got a pink ticket yet, you can get one from the office.

Oh, one more thing. I know it's summer but it can get quite cold in the mountains even in July, so bring a jacket with you. You'll need one in the evening.

All right? I'll see you tomorrow morning.

[pause]

Now listen again.

[repeat]

[pause]

This is the end of Part Five.

You now have eight minutes to write your answers on the answer sheet.

Note: Teacher, stop the recording here and time eight minutes.
Remind students when there is **one** minute remaining.

[pause]

This is the end of the test.

Test 2 Key

Paper 1   Reading and Writing

Part 1
1 D   **2** A   **3** C   **4** B   **5** E

Part 2
6 C   **7** B   **8** C   **9** B   **10** A

Part 3
11 C   **12** B   **13** A   **14** B   **15** C
16 C   **17** E   **18** G   **19** B   **20** A

Part 4
21 C   **22** B   **23** C   **24** A   **25** B   **26** C   **27** A

Part 5
28 C   **29** A   **30** A   **31** B   **32** C   **33** B   **34** C   **35** A

Part 6
Spelling must be correct.

36 book   **37** reception   **38** tent   **39** double   **40** beach

Part 7
For questions 41–50, ignore capitals/absence of capitals. Spelling must be correct.
41 last/this   **42** on   **43** a   **44** is/was   **45** have
46 am/'m   **47** you   **48** to   **49** will/can/shall/'ll   **50** opens

Part 8
For questions 51–55, spelling must be correct and capitals must be used where necessary.
51 Australian   **52** teacher   **53** Portuguese
54 Tuesday   **55** 2.30 p.m./14.30

Part 9
Question 56
The task-specific notes given below should be used in conjunction with the mark scheme for Part 9 given on page 10.

Task-specific notes
The postcard should include the following three pieces of information:

i   whether they can see Alex
ii comment about the weather
iii suggestion re: clothes.

Sample answer A

Mark: 5

All three parts of the message are communicated but there are a few errors of spelling and grammar. This is an example of a script that only just merits 5 marks.

> *Hello. Thank you for your letter. Of corse, I want to see you too.*
> *Well, My country is very cold. So you should bring many sweaters,*
> *jeanse, coats etc. I think so!!*
> *Love, Lola*

Sample answer B

Mark: 4

All three parts of the message are communicated with no need for interpretation on the part of the reader, but there are too many errors in spelling and grammar to merit a 5.

> *Hello Alex*
> *Thinks for your postcard. I love to see you. can you came in my*
> *house. The weather of my country is hot than you need to bring*
> *summer clothes.*
> *Sunny*

Sample answer C

Mark: 3

All three parts of the message have been covered but *long clothes* needs interpretation.

> *Dear Alex:*
> *Next month you can come to England see me. In England is*
> *winter now. If you come to see me you bring long clothes.*
> *Love from Valerie*

Sample answer D

Mark: 2

Only two of the points are covered and the errors are such that a considerable amount of patience is required of the reader.

> *Der Alex you are wolle comme in may contry next month I am free*
> *The weather is Bioutifoule son chain evriday.*
> *Good bay*
> *Peter*

Sample answer E

Mark: 0

This candidate only attempts one of the three points (clothes) and therefore can only be given one mark. However, they have only written 23 words and so they lose one mark because the answer is too short. Hence, the final score is zero.

> *Dear Alex*
> *I received your letter written at the back of a beautiful postcard.*
> *And you need to bring heavy clothes.*
> *Love Thomas*

Paper 2   Listening

Part 1
1 B   **2** A   **3** C   **4** B   **5** B

Part 2
6 H   **7** F   **8** A   **9** D   **10** G

Part 3
11 A   **12** B   **13** B   **14** B   **15** C

Part 4
For questions 16–20, ignore capitals/absence of capitals. In questions 18, 19 and 20, spelling must be correct.
16 two/2/one double, one single   **17** 440(.00)   **18** E A R S L E Y
19 5.30/five thirty/half past five   **20** (of) March

Part 5
For all questions, accept recognisable spelling, except number 24. Ignore capitals/absence of capitals.
21 10.45/quarter to eleven   **22** castle   **23** 8(.00)
24 park   **25** (walk to/round the old) market(s)

Transcript

This is the Key English Test. Paper 2. Listening. Test number two. There are five parts to the test. Parts One, Two, Three, Four and Five.

We will now stop for a moment before we start the test. Please ask any questions now because you mustn't speak during the test.

[pause]

PART 1   *Look at the instructions for Part One.*

[pause]

You will hear five short conversations.
You will hear each conversation twice.
There is one question for each conversation.
For questions 1–5, put a tick under the right answer.

Here is an example:
How many people were at the meeting?

Woman: Were there many people at the meeting?
Man: About thirty.
Woman: That's not many.
Man: No, but more than last time.

[pause]

The answer is 30, so there is a tick in box C.
Now we are ready to start.
Look at question one.

[pause]

Question 1 *One*
How will Mary travel to Scotland?

John: Are you taking the train to Scotland tomorrow, Mary?
Mary: No, I'm driving there, it's cheaper.
John: Why don't you go by coach?
Mary: Oh no, it takes seven hours.

[pause]

Now listen again.

[repeat]

[pause]

Question 2   *Two*
Where are the shoes?

Peter: Mum, have you seen my brown shoes?
Mother: Yes, they're under the table.
Peter: No they're not. I left them on the chair this morning, but they're not there now.
Mother: There they are – under the window!

[pause]

40

Now listen again.

[repeat]

[pause]

Question 3   *Three*

When will the football match start next week?

Tom: Does the football match start at quarter past twelve every week?
Bill: No, it was early this week. It usually begins at 2 o'clock.
Tom: So, it'll be the usual time next week?
Bill: Yes.

[pause]

Now listen again.

[repeat]

[pause]

Question 4   *Four*

Which box of chocolates do they buy?

Boy: Which box of chocolates shall we get Mum for her birthday?
Girl: Those round boxes with the flowers on are nice.
Boy: Yes, but that square box is cheaper.
Girl: But it's Mum's birthday. Let's get the big round one – we've got enough money!
Boy: OK.

[pause]

Now listen again.

[repeat]

[pause]

Question 5   *Five*

When's Wendy's birthday?

John: Wendy, you're twenty-one on Saturday, aren't you?
Wendy: No, my birthday's on May the eighteenth.
John: Well, Saturday is the eighteenth.
Wendy: No, it's not, it's the sixteenth.

[pause]

Now listen again.

[repeat]

[pause]

This is the end of Part One.

Now look at Part Two.

[pause]

PART 2   *Listen to Pete talking to a friend about his holiday.*
What was the weather like each day?
For questions 6–10, write a letter, A–H, next to each day.
You will hear the conversation twice.

[pause]

Helen: Hi Pete – you're looking well.
Pete: Yes, I've just been on holiday in the mountains for a week.
Helen: You must have had good weather.
Pete: Well, not really. When I arrived on the Monday it was very cold.
Helen: It can be cold in the mountains at this time of the year.
Pete: Yes – it wasn't very nice really. Then, on Tuesday it was so windy I just stayed in the hotel all day.
Helen: Did the weather get better?
Pete: Well, Wednesday was a bit better. There wasn't any wind and it was sunny most of the day.
Helen: So did you do a lot of walking?
Pete: No. By Thursday it was very cloudy and it looked as if it was going to snow.
Helen: And did it?
Pete: No, but on Friday it rained a lot.
Helen: And what about your last day?
Pete: Well, the weather was getting better and it was quite warm then. But it was a bit too late.

[pause]

Now listen again.

[repeat]

[pause]

This is the end of Part Two.
Now look at Part Three.

[pause]

PART 3   *Listen to Michael talking to Marina about a new sports centre.*
For questions 11–15, tick A, B or C.
You will hear the conversation twice.
Look at questions 11–15 now. You have 20 seconds.

[pause]

Now listen to the conversation.

Michael: Hello, Marina. Have you been to the new sports centre yet?
Marina: No, Michael, where is it?
Michael: In Long Road. You know, near Bridge Street, behind the station.
Marina: Oh. Is it good?
Michael: Yes, it's great! You can do a lot of sports. I played table-tennis and volleyball last week.
Marina: What about tennis?
Michael: Not yet. They're going to build some tennis courts next year.
Marina: Is it expensive?

Michael: Not really, Marina. It's £50 a year if you're 15 to 18, and £30 if you're under 15.

Marina: Oh, that's good because I'm still 14.

Michael: And on Tuesday, Thursday and Friday it stays open late – till 10 o'clock.

Marina: Oh, great. How did you get there?

Michael: I got the number 16 bus. It's only 10 minutes from the bus station. Do you want to go next week?

Marina: OK. Any day except Thursday.

Michael: Well, why don't we go on Friday? Then we can stay late.

Marina: Yes, OK. Let's meet after school.

[pause]

Now listen again.

[repeat]

[pause]

This is the end of Part Three.
Now look at Part Four.

[pause]

PART 4   *You will hear a conversation about a flat for rent.*
Listen and complete questions 16–20.
You will hear the conversation twice.

[pause]

Woman: Hello. Lonflats Agency. Can I help you?

Man: Oh yes. My name's Mark Jones. I'm phoning about the flat for rent in Putney. I saw the advertisement in the paper.

Woman: In Putney … Well, yes, Mr Jones, that one's got two bedrooms.

Man: Are they double bedrooms?

Woman: One double and one single.

Man: OK. And how much is the rent?

Woman: Well, it's £440 a month.

Man: I see. And where exactly is it?

Woman: It's number 27 Earsley Street.

Man: Oh. How do you spell that?

Woman: Earsley. It's E-A-R-S-L-E-Y. It's near the train station.

Man: And what floor is it on?

Woman: It's a second floor flat.

Man: Has it got any furniture?

Woman: Yes. It's got some nice modern furniture.

Man: Well. It sounds interesting. I'd like to see it, please.

Woman: Can you come tomorrow?

Man: Tomorrow. That's Tuesday?

Woman: Uh-hm.

Man: Well, only after 5 o'clock.

Woman: How about half past five?

Man: Yes, that's fine. Oh, one thing I nearly forgot. When will the flat be free to rent?

Woman: From the 1st of March.

Man: OK. See you tomorrow.

Woman: Bye.

[pause]

Now listen again.

[repeat]

[pause]

This is the end of Part Four.
Now look at Part Five.

[pause]

PART 5   *You will hear a tour guide talking about a day trip.*
Listen and complete questions 21–25.
You will hear the information twice.

[pause]

Guide: Hello everyone. I just want to tell you about our trip to the town of
Chester. The coach will leave at nine fifteen tomorrow morning. It takes
about an hour and a half to get to Chester, so we will arrive at a quarter
to eleven. You will have time for a cup of coffee before our first visit. This
will be to the castle. It is a very interesting old building and I'm sure you'll
enjoy the visit. Tickets for the castle cost three pounds fifty for adults and,
if you have children, a family ticket is just eight pounds. There are lots of
things to see and we will be there about two hours.
We will take sandwiches for lunch with us and we will all eat together in a
park. You will be pleased to know that tomorrow is going to be sunny.
After lunch, we will walk round the old market. You will be able to buy all
your presents there. Now, any questions?

[pause]

Now listen again.

[repeat]

[pause]

This is the end of Part Five.

You now have eight minutes to write your answers on the answer sheet.

Note: Teacher, stop the recording here and time eight minutes. Remind students
when there is **one** minute remaining.

[pause]

This is the end of the test.

Test 3 Key

Paper 1   Reading and Writing

Part 1
1 E   **2** C   **3** A   **4** G   **5** B

Part 2
6 B   **7** C   **8** A   **9** C   **10** A

Part 3
11 A   **12** B   **13** C   **14** B   **15** C
16 B   **17** F   **18** H   **19** A   **20** E

Part 4
21 B   **22** B   **23** C   **24** B   **25** A   **26** A   **27** B

Part 5
28 A   **29** B   **30** A   **31** C   **32** B   **33** B   **34** A   **35** C

Part 6
Spelling must be correct.
36 table   **37** cupboard   **38** shower   **39** window   **40** shelf

Part 7
For questions 41–50, ignore capitals/absence of capitals. Spelling must be correct.
41 to   **42** with   **43** at   **44** we   **45** this   **46** to/some
47 am/'m   **48** ask/invite/get   **49** you   **50** about

Part 8
For questions 51–55, spelling must be correct and capitals must be used where necessary.
51 23 Mount Road Oxford (England) (UK)   **52** Japanese
53 (computer) engineer   **54** (wife) Keiko (Ando)   **55** (Monday) 15(th) April

Part 9
Question 56
The task-specific notes given below should be used in conjunction with the mark scheme for Part 9 given on page 10.

Task-specific notes
The note should include the following three pieces of information:
i   invitation
ii when and
iii where the party is.

Sample answer A

Mark: 5

There is only one minor spelling error (*posible*) and all three parts of the message are communicated clearly.

> *Hi Susi*
> *Would you like to come to the party with me today? The party is in my house at 7.00pm. If you are not busy today, please call me as soon as posible.*
> *See you!*
> *Alana*

Sample answer B

Mark: 4

All the points are mentioned but there are a number of errors in spelling and grammar.

> *Dear Khalid*
> *Next weekend I'am going with my family to have party in my saster's flat an south London, and I think you like it, an if you don;'t like coming can you tell me toumorw morning.*
> *Love Halim*

Sample answer C

Mark: 3

All three points are attempted but the invitation *I'd like to come* needs interpretation.

> *Dear Jack*
> *I have a party. Today my birth day. I'd like to come. The party will be at home at 10pm. See you there.*
> *Jasmin*

Sample answer D

Mark: 2

Two points of the message are communicated but there are a considerable number of errors that require patience and interpretation by the reader.

> *Dear Nasir*
> *Please come and guinte my Barthday party at 19.6.1998. Dear Nasir you mast gunite my Barlhday party in Friday evening at 10.0 klock.*
> *Thnk you*
> *Ali   If you cant guint the party pleese contakte my on 567891*

Sample answer E

Mark: 0

The candidate has not completed the task as required and cannot be given a mark.

> *Dear friend*
> *I am come to your party. What time your party start and when I come to your party and where have your party.*
> *See you soon*
> *Boris*

Paper 2   Listening

Part 1
1 A   **2** B   **3** C   **4** A   **5** C

Part 2
6 D   **7** C   **8** F   **9** A   **10** B

Part 3
11 B   **12** C   **13** A   **14** A   **15** B

Part 4
For questions 16–19, accept recognisable spelling. Spelling needs to be correct in question 20. Ignore capitals/absence of capitals.
16 (next) Monday   **17** (about) 15/fifteen (students)
18 12.99/twelve pounds ninety-nine   **19** nine/9 (o'clock)/9 a.m. to 1 p.m.
20 Green Park

Part 5
For questions 21–25, accept recognisable spelling. Ignore capitals/absence of capitals.

21 7/seven (hours)   **22** castle   **23** café/lunch   **24** beach/lake
25 camera

Transcript

This is the Key English Test. Paper 2. Listening. Test number three. There are five parts to the test. Parts One, Two, Three, Four and Five.

We will now stop for a moment before we start the test. Please ask any questions now because you mustn't speak during the test.

[pause]

PART 1   *Look at the instructions for Part One.*

[pause]

You will hear five short conversations.
You will hear each conversation twice.
There is one question for each conversation.
For questions 1–5, put a tick under the right answer.

Here is an example:
When's the school trip?

Boy: Are you going to go on the school trip, Maria?
Girl: Yes, I am.
Boy: It's on Wednesday, isn't it?
Girl: No, on Thursday. The bus leaves at 11 o'clock.

[pause]

The answer is Thursday, so there is a tick in box C.
Now we are ready to start.
Look at question one.

[pause]

Question 1   *One*
Where's the sports centre?

Man: Excuse me. Is the sports centre near here?
Woman: Yes, it's about ten minutes' walk. Go past the bank and take the second road on the left. It's on the corner.
Man: Thanks very much.

[pause]

Now listen again.

[repeat]

[pause]

Question 2   *Two*

How much petrol does the woman want?

Woman: Could you put 30 litres of petrol in my car, please?
Man: Did you say 13 litres?
Woman: No, 30 litres. Fill it up please.

[pause]

Now listen again.

[repeat]

[pause]

Question 3   *Three*

Which table do they buy?

Woman: Look – this round table is very nice.
Man: Yes, but it's made of plastic and it's only got three legs.
Woman: Do you want one with four legs?
Man: Yes – look, here's a square one. Let's have this.
Woman: OK.

[pause]

Now listen again.

[repeat]

[pause]

Question 4   *Four*

What time does the class start?

Boy: Are you going to the English class this afternoon, Susan?
Girl: Yes, it's at three o'clock, isn't it?
Boy: Two o'clock. I've got to go to the dentist's at half past two so I can't go.
Girl: Don't worry. I'll get the homework for you.

[pause]

Now listen again.

[repeat]

[pause]

Question 5   *Five*

What was the weather like on Emma's holiday?

Man: Did you enjoy your holiday in Australia, Emma?
Emma: Yes, but it was wet most of the time.
Man: Really? Isn't it always hot in Australia?
Emma: Mm. Not when I was there.

[pause]

Now listen again.

[repeat]

[pause]

This is the end of Part One.
Now look at Part Two.

[pause]

PART 2   *Listen to Jane talking to a friend about some clothes that she has bought for her holiday. What colours are her clothes?*
For questions 6–10, write a letter, A–H, next to each of her clothes.
You will hear the conversation twice.

[pause]

Tim: Hi Jane. Have you been shopping?
Jane: Yes. I've bought some clothes. But I think I've got too many different colours.
Tim: Well, that's a nice white shirt. You can wear that with any colour.
Jane: Yes, I bought it in the same shop as this dress.
Tim: Let me see. Oh yes. What a lovely green! And have you bought a jacket to go with it?
Jane: Yes. It was difficult to find one but I finally got this dark brown one.
Tim: Oh yes – that's very nice. Did you buy anything else?
Jane: Well, I need a new sweater. I always wear this red one and it's so old now. So I bought this one.
Tim: Mmm – orange – that's an unusual colour.
Jane: Yes. I also bought a coat and some shoes.
Tim: You have been busy.
Jane: Yes. The coat was a bit expensive. Do you like it?
Tim: Oh yes. You look good in black. And those new black shoes look great with the coat.
Jane: Well, actually they're dark blue, not black.

[pause]

Now listen again.

[repeat]

[pause]

This is the end of Part Two.
Now look at Part Three.

[pause]

PART 3   *Listen to Mrs Lee talking to her secretary about her business trip.*
For questions 11–15, tick A, B or C.
You will hear the conversation twice.
Look at questions 11–15 now. You have 20 seconds.

[pause]

Now listen to the conversation.

Mrs Lee: So, tell me about my trip to Europe. Will I leave on Saturday or Sunday?
Secretary: I've booked your ticket for Saturday, Mrs Lee. Let me see, that's the 11th and your plane leaves at 10 a.m.
Mrs Lee: So, I'll get to the airport at about eight.

Secretary: Yes. And you'll arrive in London at eleven fifty – you won't stop in Frankfurt this time. Mr Porter from our Amsterdam office will arrive at about the same time, so you can go together to your meeting at the factory – no time to go to the hotel, I'm afraid.

Mrs Lee: OK. And after the meeting?

Secretary: You'll have the afternoon free. Then in the evening you'll meet Jane and Peter Cook.

Mrs Lee: Is that at their home?

Secretary: Not this time. You're going to meet in a Japanese restaurant near your hotel. Then the next morning you'll go to Paris on the train.

Mrs Lee: Yes, that's better than flying again.

[pause]

Now listen again.

[repeat]

[pause]

This is the end of Part Three.
Now look at Part Four.

[pause]

PART 4 *Listen to a man asking for some information about a language school.*
Listen and complete questions 16–20.
You will hear the conversation twice.

[pause]

Woman: Hello, School of Italian Studies.

Man: Hello, I saw your advertisement in the newspaper. Can you give me some information, please?

Woman: Yes, of course. What would you like to know?

Man: Well, first, how long are the courses?

Woman: They're six or nine months long and the next courses begin next Monday.

Man: How many students will there be in the class? Not too many, I hope.

Woman: Usually, there are about 15. We find that a good number.

Man: OK. Now, I saw the price of the course in the newspaper, but will I have to pay for anything else?

Woman: Only for the coursebook, which costs twelve pounds ninety-nine.

Man: I see. When can I come and pay?

Woman: Well, the school is open eight a.m. to seven p.m. Monday to Friday and on Saturdays from nine to one.

Man: OK. And one more question – what's the nearest underground station to your school?

Woman: It's Green Park.

Man: Green Park. I see. Well, thank you very much. Goodbye.

Woman: Goodbye.

[pause]

Now listen again.

[repeat]

[pause]

This is the end of Part Four.
Now look at Part Five.

[pause]

PART 5   *You will hear a man talking about a day trip.*
Listen and complete questions 21–25.
You will hear the information twice.

[pause]

Tour guide: Hello everybody. Tomorrow we're all going on a coach trip to Lake
Tandy and I'd just like to give you some information about the trip.
We'll be leaving here at nine thirty in the morning. It's a seven-
hour trip, so we'll be back at half past four. We're going to visit three
places. The first one is a castle. This was built six hundred years ago
and it is very interesting. After that we will stop at a café for lunch at
one o'clock. We'll stay there about three-quarters of an hour. We will
then drive on to our third stop. It will be at a beach and if you like you
can swim there or just sit in the sun and look at the scenery. The
lake is very beautiful and there are lots of birds there. So remember
to take a camera. I'm sure you'll be able to take some excellent
photographs.

[pause]

Now listen again.

[repeat]

[pause]

This is the end of Part Five.

You now have eight minutes to write your answers on the answer sheet.

Note: Teacher, stop the recording here and time eight minutes. Remind students
when there is **one** minute remaining.

[pause]

This is the end of the test.

Test 4 Key

Paper 1 Reading and Writing

Part 1
1 G   **2** B   **3** D   **4** H   **5** A

Part 2
6 A   **7** A   **8** B   **9** C   **10** C

Part 3
11 C   **12** A   **13** A   **14** A   **15** B
16 E   **17** F   **18** B   **19** H   **20** G

Part 4
21 B   **22** B   **23** A   **24** C   **25** A   **26** B   **27** A

Part 5
28 B   **29** A   **30** B   **31** A   **32** A   **33** A   **34** B   **35** C

Part 6
Spelling must be correct.
36 shoes   **37** suit   **38** raincoat   **39** shorts   **40** sweater

Part 7
For questions 41–50, ignore capitals/absence of capitals. Spelling must be correct.
41 told   **42** had/decided/have   **43** are   **44** a   **45** the   **46** were
47 me   **48** you   **49** to   **50** on/next

Part 8
For questions 51–55, spelling must be correct and capitals must be used where necessary.
51 21(st) May   **52** Paris   **53** 18.25/6.25 p.m.   **54** one/a/1/suitcase
55 clothes

Part 9
Question 56
The task-specific notes given below should be used in conjunction with the mark scheme for Part 9 given on page 10.

Task-specific notes
The note should include the following three pieces of information:

i   request to return cassette recorder
ii why you need it and
iii when you need it.

Sample answer A

Mark: 5

The three points are covered clearly and fully with only occasional grammatical errors.

> *Dear Chris*
> *Hello Chris, do you remember that I lent you my cassette*
> *recorder? Yes, I'm very sure that you can remember. But I need to*
> *use that cassette recorder. I'll use it to help me in the class*
> *because my teachers speak very fast. I'll need it on Friday. So you*
> *must bring it to me on Thursday*
> *Thank you*
> *Korin*

Sample answer B

Mark: 4

All three parts of the message are communicated with some errors in spelling and grammar.

> *Dear Chris*
> *It's well my cassette recorder? I need the cassette recorder*
> *because I have to record a cassette to Mary. i need the cassette*
> *the next week.*
> *Best whishes*
> *Rosa*

Sample answer C

Mark: 3

All three parts of the message have been attempted but *in the all in the morning* requires interpretation. There are also grammatical errors.

> *Dear Chris*
> *You have my cassette recorder, I must leave the cassette at my*
> *friend for holiday, you leave the cassette in the all in the morning,*
> *because in the afternoon, I leave the city.*
> *Thank you*
> *Mira*

Sample answer D

Mark: 3

The language is clear and accurate and would score a 5 if all three points had been included. However, the reason has been omitted.

> *Chris: Hallo, I need my cassette recorder. Could you come to my house to give it to me because I need it for today. Thank you.*

Sample answer E

Mark: 1

Only one point is communicated; the final sentence is copied from the rubric.

> *Hi Chris, yesterday I gave you my cassette recorder. I'd like that my cassette recorder return to me. And why and when you need it?*

Paper 2   Listening

Part 1
1 B   **2** A   **3** C   **4** C   **5** A

Part 2
6 B   **7** D   **8** A   **9** G   **10** H

Part 3
11 A   **12** B   **13** B   **14** A   **15** C

Part 4
For questions 16–20, ignore capitals/absence of capitals. In questions 16 and 19 spelling must be correct.
16 Friday   **17** 8.30/half past eight/eight thirty   **18** London Hotel
19 SHINDY (Street)   **20** pencil(s)

Part 5
For questions 21–24, accept recognisable spelling. Ignore capitals/absence of capitals. In question 25 spelling must be correct.
21 Midnight (Meeting)   **22** Thursday
23 (6.45 and) 9.15(p.m.) quarter past nine   **24** 2.80   **25** HAUXTON

Transcript

This is the Key English Test. Paper 2. Listening. Test number four. There are five parts to the test. Parts One, Two, Three, Four and Five.

We will now stop for a moment before we start the test. Please ask any questions now because you mustn't speak during the test.

[pause]

PART 1   *Look at the instructions for Part One.*

[pause]

You will hear five short conversations.
You will hear each conversation twice.
There is one question for each conversation.
For questions 1–5, put a tick under the right answer.

Here is an example:
What time is it?

Woman: Excuse me, can you tell me the time?
Man: Yes, it's 9 o'clock.
Woman: Thank you.
Man: You're welcome.

[pause]

The answer is nine o'clock, so there is a tick in box C.
Now we are ready to start.
Look at question one.

[pause]

Question 1 *One*

What was the weather like on Wednesday?

Woman: What was the weather like when you were on holiday?
Man: Fine; it was sunny every day until Wednesday.
Woman: Really? What happened then?
Man: Well, it was sunny in the morning, but it rained in the afternoon.

[pause]

Now listen again.

[repeat]

[pause]

Question 2 *Two*

How much did Mark's pullover cost?

Woman: That's a nice pullover, Mark – was it expensive?
Mark: Mmm. Fourteen pounds ninety-nine.
Woman: Oh, that's not bad.
Mark: No, and I do like blue.

[pause]

Now listen again.

[repeat]

[pause]

Question 3   *Three*

What did Raquel buy today?

Tina: Hi, Raquel. You're looking well. New skirt?

Raquel: Thanks Tina. No, I've had this skirt for a long time. I bought these boots
            this morning. Do you like them?

Tina: Yes, very nice. They look good with that jacket.

[pause]

Now listen again.

[repeat]

[pause]

Question 4   *Four*

How many students are there at the college?

Girl: How many students are there at your college?

Boy: Oh, there's lots. It's quite a big college.

Girl: More than three hundred?

Boy: Oh yes, more than twice that. About seven hundred and fifty, I think.

[pause]

Now listen again.

[repeat]

[pause]

Question 5   *Five*

What is David going to buy?

Woman: Hi, David. What are you looking for?

David: I don't know what to buy for Rachel's birthday.

Woman: Well, I've bought her a CD, so why don't you get her a book?

David: Yes, that's a good idea – I will.

[pause]

Now listen again.

[repeat]

[pause]

This is the end of Part One.
Now look at Part Two.

[pause]

PART 2   *Listen to Philip talking to his mother about his son, Simon.*
What is Simon going to do on Saturday and Sunday?
For questions 6–10, write a letter, A–H, next to each time of day.
You will hear the conversation twice.

[pause]

Philip: Well, Mum, thanks for having Simon to stay for a couple of days.

Mother: That's OK, Philip. What have I got to do?

Philip: Well, Saturday's busy. In the morning he's got his judo class.

Mother: Right, and in the afternoon he's going to a birthday party, isn't he?

Philip: No, that's in the evening. He's going to the football match in the afternoon, remember?

Mother: Oh yes, I remember now. So what time does the party start?

Philip: At half past seven, but Mrs Carter'll bring him home.

Mother: Fine. Now on Sunday morning, we can go to the swimming pool on our bikes.

Philip: Well, … he's got a cold, so swimming isn't a very good idea, but he'd like a bicycle ride.

Mother: OK. Your father wants to take Simon to the park in the afternoon.

Philip: Fine. And then a quiet evening watching TV.

Mother: What about a trip to the cinema?

Philip: No. I think he'll be too tired for that.

Mother: OK.

[pause]

Now listen again.

[repeat]

[pause]

This is the end of Part Two.
Now look at Part Three.

[pause]

PART 3   *Listen to Chloe talking to a man about a sailing holiday.*
For questions 11–15, tick A, B or C.
You will hear the conversation twice.
Look at questions 11–15 now. You have 20 seconds.

[pause]

Now listen to the conversation.

Man: Hello, can I help you?

Chloe: Yes, I'd like to go on a sailing holiday this summer in Italy.

Man: Have you been sailing before?

Chloe: No. I wanted to go to Sweden last year, but I didn't have enough money.

Man: Well, it is quite expensive. Sailing holidays start at about three hundred pounds.

Chloe: Yes, my friends went in August last year. They paid four hundred and fifty pounds each. The most I can pay is three hundred and eighty pounds.

Man: Well, that should be enough.

Chloe: When's the cheapest time to go?

Man: Well, August is the most expensive month. September and October are cheaper.

Chloe: October's too late for me, so I'll go in September.

Man: Would you like to be by the sea or a lake?

Chloe: Well, I'd prefer a lake in the mountains.

Man: OK. The Aqua Centre in north Italy will be best for you. That costs £370.
Chloe: OK. Can I pay by credit card? I haven't got my cheque book.
Man: Yes, that's fine.

[pause]

Now listen again.

[repeat]

[pause]

This is the end of Part Three.
Now look at Part Four.

[pause]

PART 4 *You will hear Kate and Jeremy talking about a party.*
Listen and complete questions 16–20.
You will hear the conversation twice.

[pause]

Jeremy: Hello.
Kate: Hi Jeremy. It's Kate. I'm going to have a party next week. Would you like to come to it?
Jeremy: A party – that's great. What's it for?
Kate: It's my birthday on Wednesday – I'm going to be seventeen.
Jeremy: Oh dear – I can't come on Wednesday.
Kate: No – my birthday's Wednesday, but the party's on Friday.
Jeremy: Oh, that's OK. What time will it begin?
Kate: At eight thirty.
Jeremy: Right – that should be no problem.
Kate: It's going to be at the London Hotel. Do you know where that is?
Jeremy: Let me think – the London Hotel. No, I don't.
Kate: Well, it's near the town centre on Shindy Street.
Jeremy: Could you spell that for me?
Kate: Yeah, sure. It's S-H-I-N-D-Y – Shindy Street.
Jeremy: OK. I can find that. I've got a map. Can I bring anything?
Kate: Well, I need a lot of pencils for a game we're going to play.
Jeremy: OK. I'll bring some pencils.
Kate: Thanks. See you there.

[pause]

Now listen again.

[repeat]

[pause]

This is the end of Part Four.
Now look at Part Five.

[pause]

PART 5   *You will hear some information about a cinema.*
Listen and complete questions 21–25.
You will hear the information twice.

[pause]

Woman: Thank you for calling the North London Arts Cinema, Wood Green.
There is no one to answer your call at the moment.

The North London Arts Cinema is open seven days a week, showing
a variety of British and foreign films.

Next week we will show an Italian film called *Midnight Meeting*. It is
set in Milan in the 1950s. You can see that film from Monday to
Thursday. It will be on twice a day in the evenings. That's at 6.45 and
9.15. The film lasts two hours and fifteen minutes. Tickets are £4, but
there is a special student ticket at £2.80 for all our midweek films.
Please bring your student card if you want the cheaper ticket.

The nearest car park to the cinema is in Hauxton Street. That's
H-A-U-X-T-O-N. It's just five minutes' walk from the cinema.

Thank you for calling the North London Arts Cinema. If you require
further information, phone during office hours – 9 a.m. to 4.30 p.m.,
Monday to Friday.

[pause]

Now listen again.

[repeat]

[pause]

This is the end of Part Five.

You now have eight minutes to write your answers on the answer sheet.

Note: Teacher, stop the recording here and time eight minutes. Remind the
students when there is **one** minute remaining.

[pause]

This is the end of the test.